Great Works Instructional Guides for Literature

Tuck Everlasting

A guide for the novel by Natalie Babbitt
Great Works Author: Suzanne Barchers

SHELL EDUCATION

Publishing Credits

Robin Erickson, *Production Director;* Lee Aucoin, *Creative Director;* Timothy J. Bradley, *Illustration Manager;* Emily R. Smith, M.A.Ed., *Editorial Director;* Amber Goff, *Editorial Assistant;* Don Tran, *Production Supervisor;* Corinne Burton, M.A.Ed., *Publisher*

Image Credits

Cover image Critterbiz/Piotr Wawrzyniuk/Shutterstock

Standards

© 2007 Teachers of English to Speakers of Other Languages, Inc. (TESOL)
© 2007 Board of Regents of the University of Wisconsin System. World-Class Instructional Design and Assessment (WIDA).
© Copyright 2010. National Governors Association Center for Best Practices and Council of Chief State School Officers. All rights reserved.

Shell Education

5301 Oceanus Drive
Huntington Beach, CA 92649-1030
http://www.shelleducation.com
ISBN 978-1-4258-8988-3
© 2014 Shell Educational Publishing, Inc.

Table of Contents

How to Use This Literature Guide

Today's standards demand rigor and relevance in the reading of complex texts. The units in this series guide teachers in a rich and deep exploration of worthwhile works of literature for classroom study. The most rigorous instruction can also be interesting and engaging!

Many current strategies for effective literacy instruction have been incorporated into these instructional guides for literature. Throughout the units, text-dependent questions are used to determine comprehension of the book as well as student interpretation of the vocabulary words. The books chosen for the series are complex and exemplars of carefully crafted works of literature. Close reading is used throughout the units to guide students toward revisiting the text and using textual evidence to respond to prompts orally and in writing. Students must analyze the story elements in multiple assignments for each section of the book. All of these strategies work together to rigorously guide students through their study of literature.

The next few pages will make clear how to use this guide for a purposeful and meaningful literature study. Each section of this guide is set up in the same way to make it easier for you to implement the instruction in your classroom.

Theme Thoughts

The great works of literature used throughout this series have important themes that have been relevant to people for many years. Many of the themes will be discussed during the various sections of this instructional guide. However, it would also benefit students to have independent time to think about the key themes of the novel.

Before students begin reading, have them complete *Pre-Reading Theme Thoughts* (page 13). This graphic organizer will allow students to think about the themes outside the context of the story. They'll have the opportunity to evaluate statements based on important themes and defend their opinions. Be sure to have students keep their papers for comparison to the *Post-Reading Theme Thoughts* (page 64). This graphic organizer is similar to the pre-reading activity. However, this time, students will be answering the questions from the point of view of one of the characters of the novel. They have to think about how the character would feel about each statement and defend their thoughts. To conclude the activity, have students compare what they thought about the themes before the novel to what the characters discovered during the story.

How to Use This Literature Guide (cont.)

Vocabulary

Each teacher overview page has definitions and sentences about how key vocabulary words are used in the section. These words should be introduced and discussed with students. There are two student vocabulary activity pages in each section. On the first page, students are asked to define the ten words chosen by the author of this unit. On the second page in most sections, each student will select at least eight words that he or she finds interesting or difficult. For each section, choose one of these pages for your students to complete. With either assignment, you may want to have students get into pairs to discuss the meanings of the words. Allow students to use reference guides to define the words. Monitor students to make sure the definitions they have found are accurate and relate to how the words are used in the text.

On some of the vocabulary student pages, students are asked to answer text-related questions about the vocabulary words. The following question stems will help you create your own vocabulary questions if you'd like to extend the discussion.

- How does this word describe _____'s character?
- In what ways does this word relate to the problem in this story?
- How does this word help you understand the setting?
- In what ways is this word related to the story's solution?
- Describe how this word supports the novel's theme of . . . .
- What visual images does this word bring to your mind?
- For what reasons might the author have chosen to use this particular word?

At times, more work with the words will help students understand their meanings. The following quick vocabulary activities are a good way to further study the words.

- Have students practice their vocabulary and writing skills by creating sentences and/or paragraphs in which multiple vocabulary words are used correctly and with evidence of understanding.
- Students can play vocabulary concentration. Students make a set of cards with the words and a separate set of cards with the definitions. Then, students lay the cards out on the table and play concentration. The goal of the game is to match vocabulary words with their definitions.
- Students can create word journal entries about the words. Students choose words they think are important and then describe why they think each word is important within the book.

How to Use This Literature Guide *(cont.)*

Analyzing the Literature

After students have read each section, hold small-group or whole-class discussions. Questions are written at two levels of complexity to allow you to decide which questions best meet the needs of your students. The Level 1 questions are typically less abstract than the Level 2 questions. Level 1 is indicated by a square, while Level 2 is indicated by a triangle.

These questions focus on the various story elements, such as character, setting, and plot. Student pages are provided if you want to assign these questions for individual student work before your group discussion. Be sure to add further questions as your students discuss what they've read. For each question, a few key points are provided for your reference as you discuss the novel with students.

Reader Response

In today's classrooms, there are often great readers who are below average writers. So much time and energy is spent in classrooms getting students to read on grade level, that little time is left to focus on writing skills. To help teachers include more writing in their daily literacy instruction, each section of this guide has a literature-based reader response prompt. Each of the three genres of writing is used in the reader responses within this guide: narrative, informative/explanatory, and opinion/argument. Students have a choice between two prompts for each reader response. One response requires students to make connections between the reading and their own lives. The other prompt requires students to determine text-to-text connections or connections within the text.

Close Reading the Literature

Within each section, students are asked to closely reread a short section of text. Since some versions of the novels have different page numbers, the selections are described by chapter and location, along with quotations to guide the readers. After each close reading, there are text-dependent questions to be answered by students.

Encourage students to read each question one at a time and then go back to the text and discover the answer. Work with students to ensure that they use the text to determine their answers rather than making unsupported inferences. Once students have answered the questions, discuss what they discovered. Suggested answers are provided in the answer key.

How to Use This Literature Guide *(cont.)*

Close Reading the Literature *(cont.)*

The generic, open-ended stems below can be used to write your own text-dependent questions if you would like to give students more practice.

- Give evidence from the text to support . . . .
- Justify your thinking using text evidence about . . . .
- Find evidence to support your conclusions about . . . .
- What text evidence helps the reader understand . . . ?
- Use the book to tell why _____ happens.
- Based on events in the story, ...
- Use text evidence to describe why . . . .

Making Connections

The activities in this section help students make cross-curricular connections to writing, mathematics, science, social studies, or the fine arts. In some of these lessons, students are asked to use the author as a mentor. The writing in the novel models a skill for them that they can then try to emulate. Students may also be asked to look for examples of language conventions within the novel. Each of these types of activities requires higher-order thinking skills from students.

Creating with the Story Elements

It is important to spend time discussing the common story elements in literature. Understanding the characters, setting, and plot can increase students' comprehension and appreciation of the story. If teachers discuss these elements daily, students will more likely internalize the concepts and look for the elements in their independent reading. Another very important reason for focusing on the story elements is that students will be better writers if they think about how the stories they read are constructed.

Students are given three options for working with the story elements. They are asked to create something related to the characters, setting, or plot of the novel. Students are given choice on this activity so that they can decide to complete the activity that most appeals to them. Different multiple intelligences are used so that the activities are diverse and interesting to all students.

How to Use This Literature Guide (cont.)

Culminating Activity

This open-ended, cross-curricular activity requires higher-order thinking and allows for a creative product. Students will enjoy getting the chance to share what they have discovered through reading the novel. Be sure to allow them enough time to complete the activity at school or home.

Comprehension Assessment

The questions in this section are modeled after current standardized tests to help students analyze what they've read and prepare for tests they may see in their classrooms. The questions are dependent on the text and require critical-thinking skills to answer.

Response to Literature

The final post-reading activity is an essay based on the text that also requires further research by students. This is a great way to extend this book into other curricular areas. A suggested rubric is provided for teacher reference.

Correlation to the Standards

Shell Education is committed to producing educational materials that are research and standards based. In this effort, we have correlated all of our products to the academic standards of all 50 United States, the District of Columbia, the Department of Defense Dependents Schools, and all Canadian provinces.

Purpose and Intent of Standards

Standards are designed to focus instruction and guide adoption of curricula. Standards are statements that describe the criteria necessary for students to meet specific academic goals. They define the knowledge, skills, and content students should acquire at each level. Standards are also used to develop standardized tests to evaluate students' academic progress. Teachers are required to demonstrate how their lessons meet standards. Standards are used in the development of all of our products, so educators can be assured they meet high academic standards.

How To Find Standards Correlations

To print a customized correlation report of this product for your state, visit our website at http://www.shelleducation.com and follow the online directions. If you require assistance in printing correlation reports, please contact Customer Service at 1-877-777-3450.

Correlation to the Standards (cont.)

Standards Correlation Chart

The lessons in this guide were written to support the Common Core College and Career Readiness Anchor Standards. This chart indicates which sections of this guide address the anchor standards.

Common Core College and Career Readiness Anchor Standard	Section
CCSS.ELA-Literacy.CCRA.R.1—Read closely to determine what the text says explicitly and to make logical inferences from it; cite specific textual evidence when writing or speaking to support conclusions drawn from the text.	Close Reading the Literature Sections 1–5; Culminating Activity
CCSS.ELA-Literacy.CCRA.R.2—Determine central ideas or themes of a text and analyze their development; summarize the key supporting details and ideas.	Analyzing the Literature Sections 1–5; Theme Thoughts
CCSS.ELA-Literacy.CCRA.R.3—Analyze how and why individuals, events, or ideas develop and interact over the course of a text.	Close Reading the Literature Sections 1–5; Analyzing the Literature Sections 1–5; Creating with the Story Elements Sections 1–4; Making Connections Section 2
CCSS.ELA-Literacy.CCRA.R.4—Interpret words and phrases as they are used in a text, including determining technical, connotative, and figurative meanings, and analyze how specific word choices shape meaning or tone.	Vocabulary Sections 1–5
CCSS.ELA-Literacy.CCRA.R.5—Analyze the structure of texts, including how specific sentences, paragraphs, and larger portions of the text (e.g., a section, chapter, scene, or stanza) relate to each other and the whole.	Making Connections Section 1; Creating with the Story Elements Section 4
CCSS.ELA-Literacy.CCRA.R.10—Read and comprehend complex literary and informational texts independently and proficiently.	Entire Unit
CCSS.ELA-Literacy.CCRA.W.1—Write arguments to support claims in an analysis of substantive topics or texts using valid reasoning and relevant and sufficient evidence.	Reader Response Sections 1–2, 4–5; Post-Reading Response to Literature
CCSS.ELA-Literacy.CCRA.W.2—Write informative/explanatory texts to examine and convey complex ideas and information clearly and accurately through the effective selection, organization, and analysis of content.	Reader Response Sections 2–3, 5; Culminating Activity; Post-Reading Response to Literature
CCSS.ELA-Literacy.CCRA.W.3—Write narratives to develop real or imagined experiences or events using effective technique, well-chosen details and well-structured event sequences.	Reader Response Sections 1, 3–4; Creating with the Story Elements Sections 4–5; Culminating Activity; Post-Reading Response to Literature

Correlation to the Standards (cont.)

Standards Correlation Chart (cont.)

Common Core College and Career Readiness Anchor Standard	Section
CCSS.ELA-Literacy.CCRA.W.4—Produce clear and coherent writing in which the development, organization, and style are appropriate to task, purpose, and audience.	Making Connections Section 4; Creating with the Story Elements Section 4; Culminating Activity; Post-Reading Response to Literature
CCSS.ELA-Literacy.CCRA.W.6—Use technology, including the Internet, to produce and publish writing and to interact and collaborate with others.	Making Connections Sections 3, 5
CCSS.ELA-Literacy.CCRA.W.9—Draw evidence from literary or informational texts to support analysis, reflection, and research.	Making Connections Section 5; Post-Reading Response to Literature
CCSS.ELA-Literacy.CCRA.L.1—Demonstrate command of the conventions of standard English grammar and usage when writing or speaking.	Creating with the Story Elements Section 4; Culminating Activity; Post-Reading Response to Literature
CCSS.ELA-Literacy.CCRA.L.4—Determine or clarify the meaning of unknown and multiple-meaning words and phrases by using context clues, analyzing meaningful word parts, and consulting general and specialized reference materials, as appropriate.	Vocabulary Sections 1–5
CCSS.ELA-Literacy.CCRA.L.6—Acquire and use accurately a range of general academic and domain-specific words and phrases sufficient for reading, writing, speaking, and listening at the college and career readiness level; demonstrate independence in gathering vocabulary knowledge when encountering an unknown term important to comprehension or expression.	Vocabulary Sections 1-5

TESOL and WIDA Standards

The lessons in this book promote English language development for English language learners. The following TESOL and WIDA English Language Development Standards are addressed through the activities in this book:

- **Standard 1:** English language learners communicate for social and instructional purposes within the school setting.

- **Standard 2:** English language learners communicate information, ideas and concepts necessary for academic success in the content area of language arts.

About the Author—Natalie Babbitt

Natalie Babbitt was born on July 28, 1932, in Dayton, Ohio. She spent a lot of her time as a child drawing and reading fairy tales and myths. She wanted to take after her mother and become an artist when she grew up. She even studied art in college.

After she graduated from Smith College in Massachusetts, she married Samuel Fisher Babbitt. She spent the next ten years raising her three children. During this time, she observed both her husband and her sister go through the authoring and editing process for books that they were writing. In an interview she gave for Scholastic.com, she says these years taught her some important things about writing. "You have to give writing your full attention. You have to like the revision process. And you have to like to be alone."

In 1966, Babbitt collaborated with her husband to write a children's book called *The Forty-ninth Magician*. She drew the pictures, while her husband wrote the text. After that book, her editor encouraged her to continue writing on her own. After that time, there was no stopping her. She continued to write and illustrate many popular and well-reviewed books.

One of her best-known books is *Kneeknock Rise*, which received a Newbery Honor Award in 1971. In 1975, she wrote *Tuck Everlasting*. This book was named as an American Library Association Notable book and is still popular more than 35 years later. In all, Babbitt has written 18 books and illustrated 10 other books.

In March 2013, Babbitt was awarded the very first E.B. White Award for achievement in children's literature by the American Academy of Arts and Letters.

Possible Texts for Text Comparisons

There are three other books by the author that can be used to explore Babbitt's fine character development and rich description of setting: *Kneeknock Rise*, *The Eyes of the Amaryllis*, and *Goody Hall*.

Book Summary of *Tuck Everlasting*

The Tuck family, Angus (Pa), Mae, Miles, and Jesse, are a very unusual family. They haven't changed at all for the past 87 years. A young girl named Winnie Foster, who is feeling confined by her family, sets out to explore the nearby wood. She happens upon seventeen-year-old Jesse. Then, she discovers the source of the Tuck family's secret, a small spring in the woods. When Winnie wants to drink from the spring, the Tucks realize they must stop her until she fully understands that drinking from the spring means living forever.

After kidnapping Winnie and taking her to their home, the Tucks treat Winnie kindly. They plan to return Winnie to her home the next day, after they explain everything to her. Pa Tuck talks to Winnie about how it feels to stay the same forever. He describes living as constantly changing and growing. Part of living is reaching the end of a life and dying. In contrast, his life is exactly the same every day. He doesn't get to change or grow older. He feels like the members of his family are just "rocks beside the road."

After listening to the Tucks and hearing their unusual story, she understands the consequences of drinking from the spring. Unfortunately, someone else has also heard enough of the story to cause problems for the Tuck family. The man in a yellow suit wants to take over the spring and sell the water to make himself rich.

The stranger's plans cause Mae Tuck to react violently. She accidentally kills him when she is trying to stop him. The local police officer puts Mae in jail.

Winnie decides that Mae shouldn't have to face the consequences in jail. She decides to help the Tucks break Mae out of jail. The Tucks are successful with their escape plan, and they quickly leave the area to avoid any further problems. At that point, Winnie is left alone with an incredibly hard decision to make. Will she drink from the spring when she grows up to join Jesse Tuck eternally, or will she live a normal life?

Cross-Curricular Connection

This book can be used during character education or during a literature unit on dilemmas.

Possible Texts for Text Sets

- Creech, Sharon. *Chasing Redbird*. MacMillan, 1997.
- DiCamillo, Kate. *The Miraculous Journey of Edward Tulane*. Candlewick, 2009.
- Levine, Gail Carson. *Ella Enchanted*. Harper, 2004.

Name _____

Date _____

Pre-Reading Theme Thoughts

Directions: Read each of the statements in the first column. Decide if you agree or disagree with the statements. Record your opinion by marking an *X* in Agree or Disagree for each statement. Explain your choices in the third column. There are no right or wrong answers.

Statement	Agree	Disagree	Explain Your Answer
It would be great to live forever.			
Anyone who commits a crime should be punished.			
A person should have control over his or her own life and death.			
If you have a chance to make some money, you should take it.			

Vocabulary Overview

Ten key words from this section are provided below with definitions and sentences about how the words are used in the book. Choose one of the vocabulary activity sheets (pages 15 or 16) for students to complete as they read this section. Monitor students as they work to ensure the definitions they have found are accurate and relate to the text. Finally, discuss these important vocabulary words with students. If you think these words or other words in the section warrant more time devoted to them, there are suggestions in the introduction for other vocabulary activities (page 5).

Word	Definition	Sentence about Text
tangent (ch. 1)	departure or digression	The road wandered up a hill in a **tangent**.
ambled (ch. 1)	wandered	The road **ambled** back down the hill.
tranquil (ch. 1)	quiet	The woods are **tranquil** and still.
melancholy (ch. 2)	sadness	Pa Tuck's face shows his **melancholy**.
brooch (ch. 2)	pin	Mae Tuck pins a **brooch** on her shawl.
exasperated (ch. 3)	frustrated	Winnie is **exasperated** at being told what to do all the time.
self-deprecation (ch. 4)	modesty, humility	"I'm not as pretty as you," she says with **self-deprecation**.
galling (ch. 5)	annoying	It is **galling** to Winnie to feel afraid.
instinct (ch. 5)	natural impulse, nature	Winnie's **instinct** tells her to run.
plaintively (ch. 5)	sorrowfully	Winnie **plaintively** asks to drink the water.

Name _____

Date _____

Understanding Vocabulary Words

Directions: The following words are in this section of the book. Use context clues and reference materials to determine an accurate definition for each word.

Word	Definition
tangent (ch. 1)	
ambled (ch. 1)	
tranquil (ch. 1)	
melancholy (ch. 2)	
brooch (ch. 2)	
exasperated (ch. 3)	
self-deprecation (ch. 4)	
galling (ch. 5)	
instinct (ch. 5)	
plaintively (ch. 5)	

Name _____

Date _____

During-Reading Vocabulary Activity

Directions: As you read these chapters, record at least eight important words on the lines below. Try to find interesting, difficult, intriguing, special, or funny words. Your words can be long or short. They can be hard or easy to spell. After each word, use context clues in the text and reference materials to define the word.

- _____
- _____
- _____
- _____
- _____
- _____
- _____
- _____
- _____

Directions: Respond to the questions about these words in this section.

1. How is running away a **staggering** idea in Winnie's mind?

   _____

   _____

2. What causes Granny to squint **suspiciously** at the man in the yellow suit?

   _____

   _____

Analyzing the Literature

Provided below are discussion questions you can use in small groups, with the whole class, or for written assignments. Each question is given at two levels so you can choose the right question for each group of students. Activity sheets with these questions are provided (pages 18–19) if you want students to write their responses. For each question, a few key discussion points are provided for your reference.

Story Element	■ Level 1	▲ Level 2	Key Discussion Points
Setting	Describe the woods near Winnie's home—Treegap Wood.	Why do you think no road went through Treegap? Would you feel safe exploring it?	Discuss the author's use of words that set the mood of the Treegap Wood: *sleeping, otherworld*, etc. Lead students to demonstrate understanding of how a setting can contribute to the mood of a story.
Character	Describe Mae or Pa Tuck.	Describe Mae and Pa Tuck. How are their personalities different?	Students should contrast Mae's excitement at seeing her sons with Pa Tuck's weary acceptance that nothing ever changes for them. The unchanging nature of their lives sets the stage for one of the story's dilemmas—choosing life everlasting.
Character	Describe how Winnie feels about her family.	Describe how your parents are similar to or different from Winnie's mother and Granny.	Students should begin to identify with Winnie's desire to strike out on her own.
Plot	Jesse tries to keep Winnie from drinking the water. Why?	Jesse is relieved when Mae shows up, and Mae is distressed. Why?	If students are not familiar with the plot, have them speculate on what could be so special about the water. Speculate on how the Tucks can keep Winnie away from the spring, given that it's on her father's land.

Name _____

Date _____

■ Analyzing the Literature

Directions: Think about the section you have just read. Read each question and state your response with textual evidence.

1. Describe the woods near Winnie's home—Treegap Wood.

    _____

    _____

    _____

    _____

2. Describe Mae or Pa Tuck.

    _____

    _____

    _____

    _____

3. Describe how Winnie feels about her family.

    _____

    _____

    _____

    _____

4. Jesse tries to keep Winnie from drinking the water. Why?

    _____

    _____

    _____

    _____

Name

Date

▲ Analyzing the Literature

Directions: Think about the section you have just read. Read each question and state your response with textual evidence.

1. Why do you think no road went through Treegap? Would you feel safe exploring it?

_____

_____

_____

_____

2. Describe Mae and Pa Tuck. How are their personalities different?

_____

_____

_____

_____

3. Describe how your parents are similar to or different from Winnie's mother and Granny.

_____

_____

_____

_____

4. Jesse is relieved when Mae shows up, and Mae is distressed. Why?

_____

_____

_____

Name _____

Date _____

Reader Response

Directions: Choose one of the following prompts about this section to answer. Be sure you include a topic sentence in your response, use textual evidence to support your opinion, and provide a strong conclusion that summarizes your opinion.

Writing Prompts

- **Narrative Piece**—If you met Winnie, what do you think the two of you would talk about? Tell about where and how you met her.
- **Opinion/Argument Piece**—What do you think is the most important scene in the book so far? Describe the scene and explain why you chose it.

_____

_____

_____

_____

_____

_____

_____

_____

_____

_____

_____

_____

_____

_____

Name _____

Date _____

Close Reading the Literature

Directions: Closely reread the section from the beginning of chapter four to where the cottage door opens and grandmother asks, "Winifred? Who are you talking to out there?" Read each question and then revisit the text to find the evidence that supports your answer.

1. Describe how the man in the yellow suit moves when he talks with Winnie. Give examples based on text evidence.

   _____

   _____

   _____

   _____

2. Use examples from the book to explain why Winnie decides the man is "perfectly all right."

   _____

   _____

   _____

   _____

3. Use text evidence to tell what information the man in the yellow suit is trying to learn from Winnie and her grandmother.

   _____

   _____

   _____

   _____

4. In what ways is the man in the yellow suit suspicious? Use the text to support your opinion.

   _____

   _____

   _____

   _____

Name _____

Date _____

Making Connections–Ferris Wheel

The author, Natalie Babbitt, begins the story with a description of a Ferris wheel, paused in its turning. The Ferris wheel, invented by George Ferris in 1893 for the World's Columbian Exposition in Chicago, was also known as the "observation wheel."

Directions: Reread the first paragraph of the prologue. Label the cars on this Ferris wheel with words that describe the first week of August. You can use words from the story and add your own.

Name _____

Date _____

Creating with the Story Elements

Directions: Thinking about the story elements of character, setting, and plot in a novel is very important to understanding what is happening and why. Complete **one** of the following activities about what you've read so far. Be creative and have fun!

Characters

The man in the yellow suit has no name. Make up a first, middle, and last name for him. It should match a stranger who shows up unannounced and asks many questions. Write a paragraph to justify your choice. If you need ideas, use the dictionary to look up words that describe the man or his personality.

Setting

Create a bird's-eye-view map of the Treegap Wood and Winnie's house based on what you know so far. Be detailed. You can add to the map as you continue reading.

Plot

Create a plot wheel that describes the events of the story so far. Make a list of the key events. You should have at least five. Draw a circle and divide it into the appropriate number of sections. Starting with the top section, such as 12 on a clock, write a short description of the first event. Then turn the paper and write about the next event in the order of its occurrence.

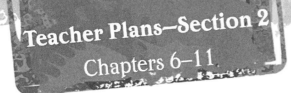
Vocabulary Overview

Ten key words from this section are provided below with definitions and sentences about how the words are used in the book. Choose one of the vocabulary activity sheets (pages 25 or 26) for students to complete as they read this section. Monitor students as they work to ensure the definitions they have found are accurate and relate to the text. Finally, discuss these important vocabulary words with students. If you think these words or other words in the section warrant more time devoted to them, there are suggestions in the introduction for other vocabulary activities (page 5).

Word	Definition	Sentence about Text
perversely (ch. 6)	rebelliously	Winnie can't think, and her mind goes **perversely** blank.
outrage (ch. 6)	horror	Winnie feels **outrage** at being kidnapped.
peculiar (ch. 7)	strange	Something **peculiar** begins to happen to the Tucks after they drink from the spring.
shamelessly (ch. 8)	boldly	Jesse shows off **shamelessly** in front of Winnie.
fantastic (ch. 8)	amazing	The man in the yellow suit listens to the **fantastic** story.
embankment (ch. 9)	ridge or bank	The path goes down a steep **embankment**.
solemnly (ch. 9)	seriously	At first, Pa Tuck greets Winnie **solemnly**.
helter-skelter (ch. 10)	disorganized	Furniture is **helter-skelter** in the Tucks' house.
luxurious (ch. 11)	lavish, expensive	Winnie thinks that eating with the Tucks is **luxurious**.
decisively (ch. 11)	determinedly	Pa Tuck insists **decisively** that they need to talk to Winnie before taking her home.

Name _____

Date _____

Understanding Vocabulary Words

Directions: The following words are in this section of the book. Use context clues and reference materials to determine an accurate definition for each word.

Word	Definition
perversely (ch. 6)	
outrage (ch. 6)	
peculiar (ch. 7)	
shamelessly (ch. 8)	
fantastic (ch. 8)	
embankment (ch. 9)	
solemnly (ch. 9)	
helter-skelter (ch. 10)	
luxurious (ch. 11)	
decisively (ch. 11)	

Name _____

Date _____

During-Reading Vocabulary Activity

Directions: As you read these chapters, record at least eight important words on the lines below. Try to find interesting, difficult, intriguing, special, or funny words. Your words can be long or short. They can be hard or easy to spell. After each word, use context clues in the text and reference materials to define the word.

- _____

- _____

- _____

- _____

- _____

- _____

- _____

- _____

- _____

- _____

Directions: Respond to the questions about these words in this section.

1. Describe what it looks like when dishes are stacked in **perilous** towers with no regard to their dimensions.

   _____

   _____

2. Describe what a **cavernous** oak wardrobe would look like.

   _____

   _____

Analyzing the Literature

Provided below are discussion questions you can use in small groups, with the whole class, or for written assignments. Each question is given at two levels so you can choose the right question for each group of students. Activity sheets with these questions are provided (pages 28–29) if you want students to write their responses. For each question, a few key discussion points are provided for your reference.

Story Element	■ Level 1	▲ Level 2	Key Discussion Points
Plot	Why does Winnie present a problem for the Tucks?	Contrast the different reactions to Winnie's presence by the members of the Tuck family.	Discuss how various emotions play out. For example, Mae is dismayed, then acts desperately. Jesse becomes excited that someone else knows the truth. Miles and Pa Tuck take time to quietly explain things in detail to Winnie.
Setting	Explain how the house is described in chapter 10.	Contrast the Tucks' house with Winnie's house.	Students should describe the clutter and casual approach to belongings of the Tucks. In contrast, Winnie's home is well-ordered and tidy.
Plot	What would it be like to have to move every few years?	Describe the problems the Tucks face because they need to remain unnoticed.	Discuss the need to move frequently, not making long-term friends, not being able to see family often, not being able to have many belongings, and so forth.
Character	How does Winnie feel when she's kidnapped?	Describe Winnie's changing emotions throughout the section.	Students should note how terrified she is when first kidnapped—though still fascinated with the experience. They should also note how she switches from feeling comfortable to homesick, understandable feelings in these circumstances. Have students speculate on how they might react.

Name _____

Date _____

■ Analyzing the Literature

Directions: Think about the section you have just read. Read each question and state your response with textual evidence.

1. Why does Winnie present a problem for the Tucks?

_____

_____

_____

_____

2. Explain how the house is described in chapter 10.

_____

_____

_____

_____

3. What would it be like to have to move every few years?

_____

_____

_____

_____

4. How does Winnie feel when she's kidnapped?

_____

_____

_____

_____

Name _____

Date _____

▲ Analyzing the Literature

Directions: Think about the section you have just read. Read each question and state your response with textual evidence.

1. Contrast the different reactions to Winnie's presence by the members of the Tuck family.

   _____

   _____

   _____

   _____

2. Contrast the Tucks' house with Winnie's house.

   _____

   _____

   _____

   _____

3. Describe the problems the Tucks face because they need to remain unnoticed.

   _____

   _____

   _____

   _____

4. Describe Winnie's changing emotions throughout the section.

   _____

   _____

   _____

   _____

Name _____

Date _____

Reader Response

Directions: Choose one of the following prompts about this section to answer. Be sure you include a topic sentence in your response, use textual evidence to support your opinion, and provide a strong conclusion that summarizes your opinion.

Writing Prompts

- **Opinion/Argument Piece**—Choose the Tuck who you feel is most like you. Describe how you're alike with evidence from the story.
- **Informative/Explanatory Piece**—Describe how the Tucks ended up in their current situation. What steps led to them having everlasting life?

_____
_____
_____
_____
_____
_____
_____
_____
_____
_____
_____
_____
_____
_____

Name _____

Date _____

Close Reading the Literature

Directions: Closely reread the section near the end of chapter ten. Begin with the paragraph that opens with, "But Mae shrugged off this observation." Read to the end of that paragraph. Read each question and then revisit the text to find the evidence that supports your answer.

1. Give evidence from the text to describe the relationship between the brothers.

   _____

   _____

   _____

   _____

2. What is Mae's philosophy on life? Determine your answer from her comments to Winnie.

   _____

   _____

   _____

   _____

3. What does Mae say about forgetting about her family's situation sometimes?

   _____

   _____

   _____

   _____

4. In what ways are the Tucks blessed and cursed? Use evidence from the story and your own beliefs to support your position.

   _____

   _____

   _____

   _____

Name _____

Date _____

Making Connections–Clutter Collage

Directions: Winnie is amazed at the clutter in the Tucks' home. She is also charmed at the notion of not worrying about cleaning up! Gather images and create a collage that includes things found in the Tucks' home. You can cut out images from magazines or newspapers. You can draw your own images, or you can print images from the Internet. Feel free to add items to the suggestions below that you'd find in a cluttered home. If you prefer, tear out the images so that your collage looks even more untidy.

cobwebs	mouse	table	cabinet	dishes	stove
lantern	spoons	forks	washtub	sofa	fireplace
armchair	rocker	brass bed	mirror	wardrobe	scraps of cloth
quilts	rugs	sewing supplies	woodworking materials	wooden soldiers	ship model
bowls	daisies and weeds	mattresses	clothes	onions	table

Name _____

Date _____

Creating with the Story Elements

Directions: Thinking about the story elements of character, setting, and plot in a novel is very important to understanding what is happening and why. Complete **one** of the following activities about what you've read so far. Be creative and have fun!

Characters

Create a Venn diagram that shows how Winnie and one of the Tucks are alike and different. Be sure to include many details from the novel to support your opinions.

Setting

Draw a bird's-eye-view of the inside of the Tucks' home, complete with all its clutter.

Plot

Recreate and complete this chart to describe what happens in chapters 6–11. Your chart should answer the questions.

What does Mae decide they have to do with Winnie?	**Why** does she make this decision?	**Where** do they go?	**Who** else knows the secret?	**What** do you think is going to happen with the man in the yellow suit?

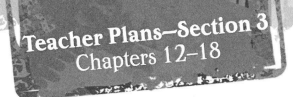

Vocabulary Overview

Ten key words from this section are provided below with definitions and sentences about how the words are used in the book. Choose one of the vocabulary activity sheets (pages 35 or 36) for students to complete as they read this section. Monitor students as they work to ensure the definitions they have found are accurate and relate to the text. Finally, discuss these important vocabulary words with students. If you think these words or other words in the section warrant more time devoted to them, there are suggestions in the introduction for other vocabulary activities (page 5).

Word	Definition	Sentence about Text
silhouettes (ch. 12)	outlines	Trees look like **silhouettes** in the fading light.
stern (ch. 12)	the back part of a boat	The **stern** of the boat is stuck against the tree.
willy nilly (ch. 12)	without planning or control	Winnie realizes she will one day die, **willy nilly**.
lingered (ch. 14)	stayed	Mae **lingered** to talk with Winnie more.
remarkable (ch. 14)	amazing	Jesse has a **remarkable** suggestion for Winnie.
destination (ch. 15)	end point of a journey	The Tucks' **destination** is their home.
illiterates (ch. 15)	unschooled people	The man in the yellow suit considers the Tucks to be **illiterates**.
constable (ch. 15)	police officer	The Fosters contact the **constable** about Winnie's disappearance.
accommodations (ch. 16)	housing, rooms	The new jailhouse provides clean **accommodations** for prisoners.
contentedly (ch. 18)	happily	Mae sighs **contentedly** while everyone eats breakfast.

Name _____

Date _____

Understanding Vocabulary Words

Directions: The following words are in this section of the book. Use context clues and reference materials to determine an accurate definition for each word.

Word	Definition
silhouettes (ch. 12)	
stern (ch. 12)	
willy nilly (ch. 12)	
lingered (ch. 14)	
remarkable (ch. 14)	
destination (ch. 15)	
illiterates (ch. 15)	
constable (ch. 15)	
accommodations (ch. 16)	
contentedly (ch. 18)	

Name _____

Date _____

During-Reading Vocabulary Activity

Directions: As you read these chapters, record at least eight important words on the lines below. Try to find interesting, difficult, intriguing, special, or funny words. Your words can be long or short. They can be hard or easy to spell. After each word, use context clues in the text and reference materials to define the word.

- _____
- _____
- _____
- _____
- _____
- _____
- _____
- _____
- _____

Directions: Now, organize your words. Rewrite each of your words on a sticky note. Work as a group to create a bar graph of your words. You should stack any words that are the same on top of one another. Different words appear in different columns. Finally, discuss with your teacher why certain words were chosen more often than other words.

Analyzing the Literature

Provided below are discussion questions you can use in small groups, with the whole class, or for written assignments. Each question is given at two levels so you can choose the right question for each group of students. Activity sheets with these questions are provided (pages 38–39) if you want students to write their responses. For each question, a few key discussion points are provided for your reference.

Story Element	■ Level 1	▲ Level 2	Key Discussion Points
Setting	Why does Pa Tuck take Winnie to the pond?	How does Pa Tuck use the pond to explain the Tucks' way of life to Winnie?	Students should explore how the boat gets stuck in the pond—just like the Tucks—and how they are like rocks.
Plot	What is the wheel of life?	Why does Pa Tuck want to get back on the wheel of life? Would you?	Students should explore the notion that life is like a wheel—going off the wheel once one has died. Students can explore Pa Tuck's despair. Remind students of the image of the Ferris wheel from the prologue.
Character	What kind of person is the man in the yellow suit?	How important do you think the man in the yellow suit is to the story? How is he affecting the plot?	Explore how the story might progress if he were not leading the constable to the Tucks' home. Have students speculate on what might happen if he retains control of the spring.
Character	What kind of person is the constable?	Contrast the constable's attitude with that of the man in the yellow suit. How are they alike and different?	Discuss how both characters want to find Winnie, but their motivations are different. Have students identify key words that describe the constable, such as *fat*, *sleepy*, etc.

Name _____

Date _____

Analyzing the Literature

Directions: Think about the section you have just read. Read each question and state your response with textual evidence.

1. Why does Pa Tuck take Winnie to the pond?

_____

_____

_____

_____

2. What is the wheel of life?

_____

_____

_____

_____

3. What kind of person is the man in the yellow suit?

_____

_____

_____

_____

4. What kind of person is the constable?

_____

_____

_____

_____

Name _____

Date _____

▲ Analyzing the Literature

Directions: Think about the section you have just read. Read each question and state your response with textual evidence.

1. How does Pa Tuck use the pond to explain the Tucks' way of life to Winnie?

_____

_____

_____

_____

2. Why does Pa Tuck want to get back on the wheel of life? Would you?

_____

_____

_____

3. How important do you think the man in the yellow suit is to the story? How is he affecting the plot?

_____

_____

_____

4. Contrast the constable's attitude with that of the man in the yellow suit. How are they alike and different?

_____

_____

_____

_____

Name _____

Date _____

Reader Response

Directions: Choose one of the following prompts about this section to answer. Be sure you include a topic sentence in your response, use textual evidence to support your opinion, and provide a strong conclusion that summarizes your opinion.

Writing Prompts

- **Informative/Explanatory Piece**—Think about the positive and negative aspects of living forever. Explain how you would feel if living forever were offered to you as a real choice.
- **Narrative Piece**—Create a new way to explain everlasting life. Think of something that can be used in the same way that Pa Tuck uses the pond. Write your description with references to the novel.

_____

_____

_____

_____

_____

_____

_____

_____

_____

_____

_____

_____

_____

_____

Name _____

Date _____

Close Reading the Literature

Directions: Closely reread the section near the end of chapter 18 when Pa Tuck says, "How'd you sleep, child?" Read to the end of the chapter. Read each question and then revisit the text to find the evidence that supports your answer.

1. Use examples from the text to describe what appeals to Winnie about staying with the Tucks.

   _____
   _____
   _____
   _____

2. Based on Winnie's thoughts in this section, do you think she is tempted to marry Jesse at age seventeen? Why or why not?

   _____
   _____
   _____
   _____

3. Describe the reaction of the Tucks to the knock at the door. Use key words drawn from the text.

   _____
   _____
   _____
   _____

4. Use text evidence to make a prediction about what is going to happen next with the man in the yellow suit.

   _____
   _____
   _____

Name _____

Date _____

Making Connections–Mosquito Math

Directions: In chapter 17, Winnie slaps at a mosquito. She thinks about how terrible it would be if all mosquitoes lived forever. Now, it's time to connect this story to mathematics. Assume that all of the mosquitoes in this problem drink from the spring.

Mosquito Life Cycle

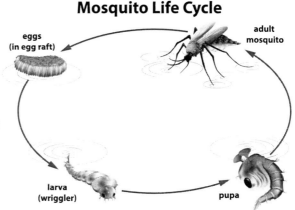

- Start with one female mosquito.
- After a month, she has a raft of 200 eggs. Half of them are female.
- About a month later those females have 200 eggs each.

1. About how many mosquitoes will have been born by the end of the second month?

   _____

2. About how many months does it take to get over a million mosquitoes?

   _____

3. Write your own math mosquito question. (Record your answer on the back of this page so that you can challenge a classmate to solve your problem.)

   _____

   _____

   _____

   _____

   _____

Bonus

Use the Internet or other references to find out why only female mosquitoes draw blood.

   _____

   _____

Name _____

Date _____

Creating with the Story Elements

Directions: Thinking about the story elements of character, setting, and plot in a novel is very important to understanding what is happening and why. Complete **one** of the following activities about what you've read so far. Be creative and have fun!

Characters

Draw a picture of the constable based on the description of him in this section. If you would prefer, draw a word picture where you use key words from the story and their synonyms. Write the words in an artistic way to create the picture.

Setting

Recreate this word splash to describe the pond near the Tucks' home. Write **pond** in the middle. Use key words from the description of the pond and your own visualizations. Then, "splash," or write these descriptive words around the page.

Plot

Recreate this problem-solution chart for the Tucks. Write a description of the main problem on the left. Write three or more possible solutions on the right.

Problem	Possible Solutions

Vocabulary Overview

Ten key words from this section are provided below with definitions and sentences about how the words are used in the book. Choose one of the vocabulary activity sheets (page 45 or 46) for students to complete as they read this section. Monitor students as they work to ensure the definitions they have found are accurate and relate to the text. Finally, discuss these important vocabulary words with students. If you think these words or other words in the section warrant more time devoted to them, there are suggestions in the introduction for other vocabulary activities (page 5).

Word	Definition	Descriptive Sentence
philosophy (ch. 19)	attitude, way of thinking	People can study **philosophy**, which gives different viewpoints about life.
tension (ch. 19)	stress, strain	The Tucks regularly experience **tension**.
ghastly (ch. 19)	frightening	The man in the yellow suit has a **ghastly** smile.
unflinchingly (ch. 20)	bravely	Winnie defends the Tucks **unflinchingly**.
exertion (ch. 22)	effort	It is so hot that any **exertion** is tiring.
prostrate (ch. 23)	drained	The **prostrate** group finds breathing hard in the heat.
furrowed (ch. 24)	wrinkled	Mae's brows are **furrowed** as she concentrates.
exultant (ch. 24)	jubilant, joyful	Jesse gives an **exultant** laugh.
accomplice (ch. 25)	collaborator, helper	Winnie is happy to be an **accomplice** to the Tucks.
custody (ch. 25)	safekeeping	Winnie prefers being in the **custody** of her family to being in the jailhouse.

Name _____

Date _____

Understanding Vocabulary Words

Directions: The following words are in this section of the book. Use context clues and reference materials to determine an accurate definition for each word.

Word	Definition
philosophy (ch. 19)	
tension (ch. 19)	
ghastly (ch. 19)	
unflinchingly (ch. 20)	
exertion (ch. 22)	
prostrate (ch. 23)	
furrowed (ch. 24)	
exultant (ch. 24)	
accomplice (ch. 25)	
custody (ch. 25)	

Name _____

Date _____

During-Reading Vocabulary Activity

Directions: As you read these chapters, record at least eight important words on the lines below. Try to find interesting, difficult, intriguing, special, or funny words. Your words can be long or short. They can be hard or easy to spell. After each word, use context clues in the text and reference materials to define the word.

- _____
- _____
- _____
- _____
- _____
- _____
- _____
- _____
- _____

Directions: Respond to the questions about these words in this section.

1. How does the word **petulance** fit the man in the yellow suit when he is trying to convince the Tucks to go along with his plans for the spring?

   _____

   _____

2. How do you know that the Fosters place a high value on **gentility**?

   _____

   _____

Analyzing the Literature

Provided below are discussion questions you can use in small groups, with the whole class, or for written assignments. Each question is given at two levels so you can choose the right question for each group of students. Activity sheets with these questions are provided (pages 48–49) if you want students to write their responses. For each question, a few key discussion points are provided for your reference.

Story Element	■ Level 1	▲ Level 2	Key Discussion Points
Plot	Does Mae do the right thing in trying to stop the man in the yellow suit? Why or why not?	What other options does Mae have for stopping the man in the yellow suit? Is she justified in her choice?	Discuss whether anyone is justified in killing another person and what might have happened had the man lived. Come up with alternatives for solving the problem of discovery.
Character	How does Winnie show that she is brave?	Contrast Mae's act of courage to Winnie's. Who is more brave, and why?	Discuss how each person is defending people they care about. Winnie is courageous for such a young person. In the past, Mae generally has taken the lead with her family.
Setting	What role does the weather play in the story?	What factors contribute to the success of Mae's escape?	Discuss how the Tucks take advantage of the construction of the jailhouse, the noise of the storm, and Winnie's help for Mae's escape.
Plot	Why does Winnie pour the spring water on the toad? Would you have done that? Why or why not?	Winnie uses up the spring water on the toad knowing she can get more at age 17. Do you think she will? What would you do?	Discuss the dilemma Winnie faces with her worry about the toad and about her decision regarding Jesse. Speculate as to what will happen next.

Name _____

Date _____

■ Analyzing the Literature

Directions: Think about the section you have just read. Read each question and state your response with textual evidence.

1. Does Mae do the right thing in trying to stop the man in the yellow suit? Why or why not?

_____

_____

_____

_____

2. How does Winnie show that she is brave?

_____

_____

_____

_____

3. What role does the weather play in the story?

_____

_____

_____

4. Why does Winnie pour the spring water on the toad? Would you have done that? Why or why not?

_____

_____

_____

_____

Name _____

Date _____

Analyzing the Literature

Directions: Think about the section you have just read. Read each question and state your response with textual evidence.

1. What other options does Mae have for stopping the man in the yellow suit? Is she justified in her choice?

_____

_____

_____

_____

2. Contrast Mae's act of courage to Winnie's. Who is more brave, and why?

_____

_____

_____

_____

3. What factors contribute to the success of Mae's escape?

_____

_____

_____

_____

4. Winnie uses up the spring water on the toad knowing she can get more at age 17. Do you think she will? What would you do?

_____

_____

_____

Name _____

Date _____

Reader Response

Directions: Choose one of the following prompts about this section to answer. Be sure you include a topic sentence in your response, use textual evidence to support your opinion, and provide a strong conclusion that summarizes your opinion.

Writing Prompts

- **Opinion Piece**—What are two questions that you would like to ask Winnie about her choices at the end of the book? Why did you choose each question?
- **Narrative Piece**—Before you read the author's epilogue, write one yourself. What happens to Winnie and the Tuck family after chapter 25?

_____

_____

_____

_____

_____

_____

_____

_____

_____

_____

_____

_____

_____

_____

_____

_____

Name _____

Date _____

Close Reading the Literature

Directions: Closely reread the first four paragraphs of chapter 23. Read each question and then revisit the text to find the evidence that supports your answer.

1. Describe the role of the sun in the first paragraph. Use your own words, but draw upon the description in the text.

   _____

   _____

   _____

   _____

2. In the second paragraph, Winnie finds her mother and grandmother more interesting. Why? Give examples from the text to support your reasons.

   _____

   _____

   _____

   _____

3. Based on Winnie's thoughts, why is she happy to go to supper even though she isn't hungry?

   _____

   _____

   _____

   _____

4. How does the author use colors in the text to create and change the mood in the third paragraph?

   _____

   _____

   _____

   _____

Name _____

Date _____

Making Connections–Wanted!

Directions: Create wanted posters for two memebers of the Tuck family. Include the following information on each poster.

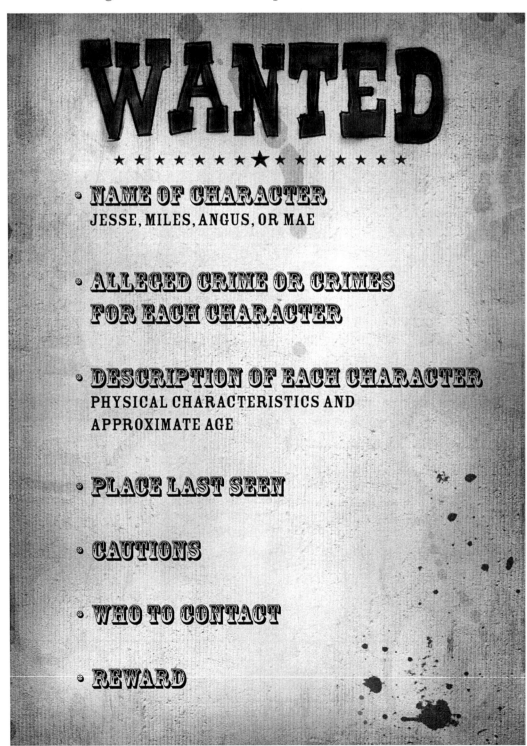

WANTED

★ ★ ★ ★ ★ ★ ★ ★ ★ ★ ★ ★ ★ ★ ★

- **NAME OF CHARACTER**
  JESSE, MILES, ANGUS, OR MAE

- **ALLEGED CRIME OR CRIMES FOR EACH CHARACTER**

- **DESCRIPTION OF EACH CHARACTER**
  PHYSICAL CHARACTERISTICS AND APPROXIMATE AGE

- **PLACE LAST SEEN**

- **CAUTIONS**

- **WHO TO CONTACT**

- **REWARD**

Name _____

Date _____

Creating with the Story Elements

Directions: Thinking about the story elements of character, setting, and plot in a novel is very important to understanding what is happening and why. Complete **one** of the following activities about what you've read so far. Be creative and have fun!

Characters

Make a list of jobs that the Tucks could do that would take advantage of their being invincible. What jobs or activities would you like to do if you knew you couldn't get hurt? Explain why you'd want to take on each job or activity.

Setting

Create a board game based on the setting of *Tuck Everlasting*. For example, a path could start at the spring, wind through the Treegap Wood, to the Tucks' house, to the jailhouse, and end at the Fosters' house. Write a set of at least 15 game cards. Each card should have a question about the story and the number of squares one advances for each correct answer. If you prefer, you can model your game after one that you enjoy playing as long as it suits the story.

Plot

Write a chapter that tells what happens if Mae is hanged. Mae can't die, which presents the Tucks with another dilemma. How do the Tucks cover up, cope, or run away again?

Vocabulary Overview

Ten key words from this section are provided below with definitions and sentences about how the words are used in the book. Choose one of the vocabulary activity sheets (page 55 or 56) for students to complete as they read this section. Monitor students as they work to ensure the definitions they have found are accurate and relate to the text. Finally, discuss these important vocabulary words with students. If you think these words or other words in the section warrant more time devoted to them, there are suggestions in the introduction for other vocabulary activities (page 5).

Word	Definition	Descriptive Sentence
epilogue	conclusion	The **epilogue** wraps up the story about Winnie and the Tucks.
blacktopped	road surface of asphalt	The road through Treegap is **blacktopped**.
continuous	constant	For most people, change is **continuous**.
catholic	varied	The village has a **catholic** group of houses.
verandah	porch	The building has a pleasant **verandah**.
chrome	shiny metal finish	The **chrome** gleams in the diner.
linoleum	floor covering	The diner has **linoleum** floors.
orangeade	drink made with orange juice	**Orangeade** is kept in a cooler.
curlicues	curls in a design	The gates to the cemetery have **curlicues**.
bulldoze	flatten	After the tree was hit by lightning, they had to **bulldoze** the area.

(All of these words are found in the epilogue.)

Name _____

Date _____

Understanding Vocabulary Words

Directions: The following words are in this section of the book. Use context clues and reference materials to determine an accurate definition for each word.

Word	Definition
epilogue	
blacktopped	
continuous	
catholic	
verandah	
chrome	
linoleum	
orangeade	
curlicues	
bulldoze	

(All of these words are found in the epilogue.)

Name _____

Date _____

During-Reading Vocabulary Activity

Directions: As you read these chapters, choose five important words from the story. Use these words to complete the word flow chart below. On each arrow, write a word. In each box, explain how the connected pair of words relates to each other. An example for the words *epilogue* and *blacktopped* has been done for you.

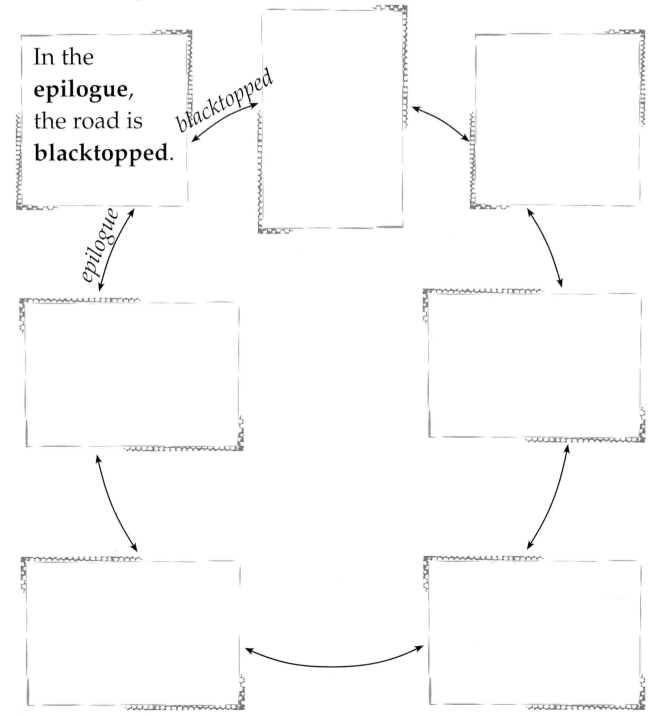

In the **epilogue**, the road is **blacktopped**.

blacktopped

epilogue

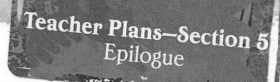

Analyzing the Literature

Provided below are discussion questions you can use in small groups, with the whole class, or for written assignments. Each question is given at two levels so you can choose the right question for each group of students. Activity sheets with these questions are provided (pages 58–59) if you want students to write their responses. For each question, a few key discussion points are provided for your reference.

Story Element	■ Level 1	▲ Level 2	Key Discussion Points
Setting	What has happened to the Fosters' home? How do the Tucks feel?	Describe why the Tucks are shocked and saddened by the disappearance of the Fosters' home.	The Tucks may be hoping that Winnie used the spring water. Discuss the emotional connection to the area, contrasted with their need to move on routinely due to their lack of aging.
Characters	Why does the man by the Hudson automobile refer to the Tucks as being in town from the country?	Should the Tucks try to keep up with times instead of continuing to use a horse and wagon?	Students may feel that the Tucks should keep up so that they are less noticeable. At the same time, the Tucks discovered long ago not to worry if they look old-fashioned. The conflict of not caring about appearances while wanting to remain anonymous presents an interesting conundrum.
Plot	When Pa Tuck realizes that Winnie chose a normal life, he says, "Good girl." Why?	How do the words *mixed emotions* apply to the feelings of the Tucks when they find Winnie's grave?	Pa Tuck believes that she made the right choice. Yet, they enjoyed having her as part of the family. Also, it would have made Jesse happy to have her as a wife, even though those days had long passed.
Plot	Would you have chosen to drink the water? Why or why not?	Discuss the pros and cons of drinking the water. If you were near death after a long, happy life, would you want to drink some just to "buy some time"?	Discuss the challenges of making a difficult decision as a young person—and how it can be just as difficult for an adult. Students may bring up religion as a way of achieving eternal life, contrasting it with life on Earth.

Name _____

Date _____

Analyzing the Literature

Directions: Think about the section you have just read. Read each question and state your response with textual evidence.

1. What has happened to the Fosters' home? How do the Tucks feel?

   _____

   _____

   _____

   _____

2. Why does the man by the Hudson automobile refer to the Tucks as being in town from the country?

   _____

   _____

   _____

3. When Pa Tuck realizes that Winnie chose a normal life, he says, "Good girl." Why?

   _____

   _____

   _____

   _____

4. Would you have chosen to drink the water? Why or why not?

   _____

   _____

   _____

   _____

▲ Analyzing the Literature

Directions: Think about the section you have just read. Read each question and state your response with textual evidence.

1. Describe why the Tucks are shocked and saddened by the disappearance of the Fosters' home.

_____

_____

_____

_____

2. Should the Tucks try to keep up with times instead of continuing to use a horse and wagon?

_____

_____

_____

3. How do the words mixed emotions apply to the feelings of the Tucks when they find Winnie's grave?

_____

_____

_____

4. Discuss the pros and cons of drinking the water. If you were near death after a long, happy life, would you want to drink some just to "buy some time"?

_____

_____

_____

Name _____

Date _____

Reader Response

Directions: Choose one of the following prompts about this section to answer. Be sure you include a topic sentence in your response, use textual evidence to support your opinion, and provide a strong conclusion that summarizes your opinion.

Writing Prompts

- **Informative/Explanatory Piece**—What is something that you think about differently now that you have read this book? Explain how your thoughts changed.
- **Opinion Piece**—Pick a scene in which you disagree with how Winnie handles a situation. Describe how you would change the scene.

_____

_____

_____

_____

_____

_____

_____

_____

_____

_____

_____

_____

_____

_____

Name _____

Date _____

Close Reading the Literature

Directions: Closely reread the last three paragraphs of the epilogue. Read each question and then revisit the text to find the evidence that supports your answer.

1. Think about the role of the toad throughout the story. In this scene, why is the toad unconcerned about getting run over?

   _____

   _____

   _____

   _____

   _____

2. Why do you think Pa Tuck makes sure the toad is safe? Give your answer based on the events in the story and your own opinion about Pa.

   _____

   _____

   _____

   _____

   _____

3. Why do you think the author ends the story with the tinkling of the music box? Think about the author's style of writing and the role of the music box in the story.

   _____

   _____

   _____

   _____

   _____

   _____

Name _____

Date _____

Making Connections–All About Toads

Directions: The toad plays an interesting role in this novel. How much do you really know about toads? For example do you know the answers to these questions? How are a frog and a toad alike and different? Do toads really drink water through their skin like Winnie's grandma says? Research this interesting amphibian to learn facts about what it looks like, its life cycle, and what it eats. While doing your research, make note of common misconceptions about frogs and toads.

1. Create a graphic organizer in the space below to share what you've learned about toads. Be sure that the visual you use for your graphic organizer makes sense for the information that you're going to share.

2. What is at least one key misconception about frogs or toads?

_____

_____

Name _____

Date _____

Creating with the Story Elements

Directions: Thinking about the story elements of character, setting, and plot in a novel is very important to understanding what is happening and why. Complete **one** of the following activities about what you've read so far. Be creative and have fun!

Characters

Winnie wants to make a difference in the world. She made a great difference in the lives of the Tucks, preventing them from being found out. What would you like to do to make a difference for your family, friends, or in your world? Write about at least one short-term and one long-term goal.

Setting

If the spring hadn't been bulldozed, the Tucks might face another dilemma. Choose a partner and debate whether they should try to destroy the spring themselves. One of you should take the position that nature should not be tampered with— that the spring was obviously there for a reason. The other should take the position that the spring is *not* normal and that it interferes with the circle of life.

Plot

Write a scene that describes what would have happened if the Tucks had come to Treegap a few years before Winnie died. What would they have talked about? How would they have felt? How would Winnie and her family have felt?

Name _____

Date _____

Post-Reading Theme Thoughts

Directions: Read each of the statements in the first column. Choose a main character from *Tuck Everlasting*. Think about that character's point of view. From that character's perspective, decide if the character would agree or disagree with the statements. Record the character's opinion by marking an X in Agree or Disagree for each statement. Explain your choices in the third column using text evidence.

Character I Chose: _____

Statement	Agree	Disagree	Explain Your Answer
It would be great to live forever.			
Anyone who commits a crime should be punished.			
A person should have control over his or her own life and death.			
If you have a chance to make some money, you should take it.			

Name _____

Date _____

Culminating Activity: Treegap Revisited

Overview: The story of the Tucks actually begins before the opening pages. When Jessie meets Winnie in 1880, he has lived 104 years, having drunk from the spring 87 years before at age 17. The descriptions of the setting of Treegap are woven into the plot, providing context for what changes—and what stays the same.

Directions: Complete the chart with descriptions of Treegap from when the Tucks first discovered the spring (1793), from when Winnie lived (1880), and from when Mae and Pa Tuck returned (1950). Suggestions for relevant chapters are provided. You can also do some online research to find out what was happening in the United States during those times.

Treegap in 1793 (See chapter 7.)	Treegap in 1880 (See chapter 1.)	Treegap in 1950 (See epilogue.)

Directions: Imagine what Treegap looks like now. Draw and write your description.

_____

_____

_____

_____

_____

_____

_____

Name _____

Date _____

Culminating Activity: Treegap Revisited (cont.)

Directions: The setting in *Tuck Everlasting* is critical to the story. After completing the chart for *Treegap Revisited*, choose from one of these culminating projects:

Design three stage sets that show Treegap in 1793, 1880, and 1950. You can represent the staging through dioramas or labeled drawings. Make the sets detailed so that it's clear what you have imagined for each setting.

Create a travel brochure that advertises Treegap as a place to visit to not only enjoy the Treegap Wood, but to obtain the magical spring water. Create it as if the man in the yellow suit had lived and were still in control of the spring today.

Set the stage for a sequel by thinking of a way that the spring could reappear in present day: an earthquake, landslide, flood, and so forth. Assume that you are the only person who knows about the powers of the spring. As someone who also wants to make a difference in the world, what would you do? Write about your choices and justify them.

Name _____

Date _____

Comprehension Assessment

Directions: Circle the letter for the best response to each question.

1. What is unusual about Winnie's kidnapping?

    a. Jesse wants Winnie to grow up and marry him.

    b. The Tucks want Winnie to join their family.

    c. The Tucks have Winnie's best interests at heart.

    d. The Tucks are seen taking her by the man in the yellow suit.

2. How do the Tucks *confirm* that they are unchanged due to the spring?

    e. The cat has died, but the horse lives even after being shot.

    f. Jesse isn't hurt when he falls out of a tree.

    g. Miles's wife leaves him because he hasn't aged.

    h. During a return visit, the clearing, spring, and carving on the tree are unchanged.

3. Write the main idea of the text below in the graphic organizer.

    "'All right,' said Winnie. For, she decided, there wasn't any choice. She would have to go. They would probably make her go, anyway, no matter what she said. But she felt there was nothing to be afraid of, not really. For they seemed gentle. Gentle and—in a strange way—childlike. They made her feel old. And the way they spoke to her, the way they looked at her, made her feel special."

Main Idea (question 3)

Details (question 4)

Details (question 4)

Name _____

Date _____

Comprehension Assessment (cont.)

4. Choose two supporting details from those below to add to the graphic organizer on the previous page.

   a. The Tucks are kind and care about Winnie.

   b. The man in the yellow suit is looking for Winnie.

   c. Winnie feels more grown up with the Tucks.

   d. Winnie's family would look for her.

5. Which statement best expresses a theme of the book?

   e. People sometimes face difficult choices.

   f. People should always be punished for crimes, no matter what the reasons.

   g. Children should be allowed freedom to explore and face danger.

   h. Becoming rich is worth whatever you have to do.

6. What detail from the book provides the best evidence for your answer to number 5?

   a. "They'll hang her for sure."

   b. "I want the wood and you want the child."

   c. "Mae had done what she thought she had to do."

   d. "She was running away, after all . . . ."

7. What is the purpose of this sentence from the book: "People got to do something useful if they're going to take up space in the world."

   _____

   _____

   _____

8. Which other quotation from the story serves a similar purpose?

   e. "She was released, then, into the custody of her mother and father."

   f. "He put his arms around her and hugged her tight, and whispered the single word, 'Remember!'"

   g. "I'm not exactly sure what I'd do, you know, but something interesting, something that's all mine."

   h. "She would never forget the rattle of the rain on the jailhouse roof, or the smell of wet wood . . . ."

Name _____

Date _____

Response to Literature: You Decide!

Overview: *Tuck Everlasting* presents a number of questions to think about:

- Would you really want to live forever?

- Are some crimes justifiable?

- Should people have control over when they die?

- If you see an opportunity to make money, should you take it, no matter what the consequences?

The man in the yellow suit justifies his plans for the spring, saying, "But I'm not going to sell it to just anybody. Only to certain people, people who deserve it. And it will be very, very expensive."

Directions: Assume that the man in the yellow suit gained control of the spring. Once a month, he rules on who will be granted the right to drink from the spring. So that the world doesn't get overpopulated, he chooses just one person each month. Write a report on the following candidates that explores whether each should have the right to drink from the spring. Your report should explore the pros and cons of each candidate's potential as the chosen recipient. Conclude with your choice, summarizing how you came to that choice.

- Candidate A is a brilliant physicist who has won awards for her inventions. She is elderly with limited time to live. However, her mind is still sharp. If allowed to live, she could perhaps find the cure for cancer. She also could invent chemical weapons that could destroy the world—and the spring. She has enough money to pay for the spring water.

- Candidate B, a decorated war hero, has been charged with the assassination of the president of a powerful enemy country. He claims he is innocent. The United States has been at war with this country in the past. Now, the enemy country insists that the alleged assassin be put to death. Candidate B wants to live so that he can prove his innocence. He has enough money to pay for the spring water, but he may have gotten the money as payment for the assassination.

- Candidate C has a terminal disease. Without the spring water, this candidate will live no more than six months. The candidate is a talented artist, who is only ten years old. His parents have raised the money for the spring water. The child is wheelchair bound and will always need help getting around—forever, if the child receives the spring water. Also, the child will be essentially frozen in time—ten years old forever.

Name _____

Date _____

Response to Literature Rubric

Directions: Use this rubric to evaluate student responses.

	Exceptional Writing	**Quality Writing**	**Developing Writing**
Focus and Organization	☐ States a clear opinion and elaborates well. Engages the reader from hook through the middle to the conclusion. Demonstrates clear understanding of the intended audience and purpose of the piece.	☐ Provides a clear and consistent opinion. Maintains a clear perspective and supports it through elaborating details. Makes the opinion clear in the opening hook and summarizes well in the conclusion.	☐ Provides an inconsistent point of view. Does not support the topic adequately or misses pertinent information. Provides lack of clarity in the beginning, middle, and conclusion.
Text Evidence	☐ Provides comprehensive and accurate support. Includes relevant and worthwhile text references.	☐ Provides limited support. Provides few supporting text references.	☐ Provides very limited support for the text. Provides no supporting text references.
Written Expression	☐ Uses descriptive and precise language with clarity and intention. Maintains a consistent voice and uses an appropriate tone that supports meaning. Uses multiple sentence types and transitions well between ideas.	☐ Uses a broad vocabulary. Maintains a consistent voice and supports a tone and feelings through language. Varies sentence length and word choices.	☐ Uses a limited and unvaried vocabulary. Provides an inconsistent or weak voice and tone. Provides little to no variation in sentence type and length.
Language Conventions	☐ Capitalizes, punctuates, and spells accurately. Demonstrates complete thoughts within sentences, with accurate subject-verb agreement. Uses paragraphs appropriately and with clear purpose.	☐ Capitalizes, punctuates, and spells accurately. Demonstrates complete thoughts within sentences and appropriate grammar. Paragraphs are properly divided and supported.	☐ Incorrectly capitalizes, punctuates, and spells. Uses fragmented or run-on sentences. Utilizes poor grammar overall. Paragraphs are poorly divided and developed.

The responses provided here are just examples of what students may answer. Many accurate responses are possible for the questions throughout this unit.

During-Reading Vocabulary Activity—Section 1: Chapters 1–5 (page 16)

1. The word **staggering** describes Winnie's feelings
of daring and shock because she's led such a
confined life.

2. Granny is startled by the man's yellow suit, and she doesn't recognize him, which makes her look at him **suspiciously**.

Close Reading the Literature—Section 1: Chapters 1–5 (page 21)

1. The man gestures self-deprecatingly with his fingers, taps his foot, twitches his shoulders, moving both in jerks and gracefully. He seems to hang like a marionette.

2. The man has a friendly and agreeable smile. He seems polite and casual.

3. The man wants to know how long Winnie's family has lived there and whether they know about everything that goes on. He wants to know if they see who comes and goes.

4. Students may note that he asks a lot of questions, he seems to sneak around, and he's very smooth. On the other hand, he is friendly, thoughtful, and quiet-spoken.

During-Reading Vocabulary Activity—Section 2: Chapters 6–11 (page 26)

1. The dishes are stacked haphazardly, thus **perilously** close to falling.

2. A **cavernous** wardrobe would be huge, with space for storage.

Close Reading the Literature—Section 2: Chapters 6–11 (page 31)

1. From reading the chapter, students know that Jesse talks with excitement about the things they've seen and will see while Miles talks more seriously about the realities of their lives. Jesse's youth affects his outlook on things, yet they enjoy certain things together, such as swimming in the pond. In general, Mae says, they don't get along very well and they go their separate ways.

2. Mae says that life has to be lived, that you have to take what comes, living one day at a time.

3. Mae comments that she wonders why it happened to them—that they are "plain as salt."

4. Living forever could be considered a blessing because you get to see so much, and you don't have to worry about dying or becoming sick. On the other hand, the Tucks have to keep moving, can't enjoy a normal way of life, can't develop lifelong friends, etc.

Close Reading the Literature—Section 3: Chapters 12–18 (page 41)

1. Winnie likes the family members. She is intrigued with Jesse and is very fond of Pa Tuck. The untidy house is appealing, perhaps because it's so different from her home.

2. Winnie thinks about staying and marrying Jesse when she is 17, so she is probably tempted to be with him. She also likes the family.

3. The sound of the knock is *alien*, *sudden*, and *surprising*. Mae drops her fork and everyone looks *startled*.

4. Some students might be inclined to trust him because he's so polite. On the other hand, some students might not trust him believing that he must have an ulterior motive—that he's *too* polite.

Making Connections—Section 3: Chapters 12–18 (page 42)

1. 20,000 mosquitoes (only 10,000 are female)

2. By the third month, there would be well over a million mosquitoes born.

3. Students will write their own questions and answers.

Bonus: Females need protein for the eggs they are going to have.

During-Reading Vocabulary Activity—Section 4: Chapters 19–25 (page 46)

1. The man in the yellow suit is annoyed and nervous when the Tucks will not agree to his scheme, showing **petulance** in his voice.

2. Winnie's mother and grandmother value a tidy house, doing things correctly, and ensuring that Winnie behaves, all contributing to their love of **gentility**.

Close Reading the Literature—Section 4: Chapters 19–25 (page 51)

1. The sun makes it so hot that people have no energy. The suns seems to "roar without a sound" and has a "blazing glare." Even the curtains can't keep it out.

2. Winnie finds them more interesting because they aren't acting as proper and genteel as usual. Their hair isn't as tidy, and they sit loosely.

3. Time is moving too slowly for Winnie. She can't even concentrate on reading. Having dinner is at least something to do.

4. She writes about how the sky changes from blue to a haze, and then writes about how the haze hardens to brownish-yellow. The leaves of the trees have a silvery cast. The colors help you see how hot and oppressive the air is and what a relief the rain would be.

Making Connections—Section 4: Chapters 19–25 (page 52)

Posters will vary, but should have the listed elements: names, crimes, descriptions, place last seen, cautions, contact person, and reward.

Close Reading the Literature—Section 5: Epilogue (page 61)

1. The toad, over time, must have realized that it can't be harmed because it had the spring water poured on it. It is a symbol of Winnie's respect for life.

2. Pa Tuck is a kind man, placing value on all life, respecting the cycle of life and how things should happen naturally.

3. The author uses the music box to signal the presence of the Tucks. The author may have chosen it because it is a precious item that could last for hundreds of years and be carried by Mae. Also, the writing throughout the story is lyrical—much like music.

Comprehension Assessment (pages 67–68)

1. c. The Tucks have Winnie's best interests at heart.

2. h. During a return visit, the clearing, spring, and carving on the tree are unchanged.

3. Main idea: Winnie is not afraid because she likes the Tucks.

4. Supporting Details: a. The Tucks are kind and care about Winnie. c. Winnie feels more grown up with the Tucks.

5. a. People sometimes face difficult choices.

6. g. "Mae had done what she thought she had to do."

7. Possible answers include that people need to contribute or that people should try to help others or make a positive difference.

8. c. "'I'm not exactly sure what I'd do, you know, but something interesting, something that's all mine.'"